FORGING DISCIPLINE

12 MONTHS. 12 CHALLENGES. 1 BADASS YOU.

JOSH MATHE

MOUNTAIN
INNA
PUBLISHING

ALSO BY JOSH MATHE

In the Footsteps of Greatness: One man's journey to conquer his demons - and the entire 2 1 2 mile John Muir Trail along the way

I, Athlete: How to unleash your inner athlete and supercharge your life

Stop Nail Biting For Good: 1 0 simple steps you can implement today

FORGING DISCIPLINE
12 MONTHS. 12 CHALLENGES. 1 BADASS YOU.

Copyright © 2021 by Josh Mathe

SPECIAL INVITATION

To my amazing readers:

Thank you for picking up this book and reading it! As a thank you I'd like to give you a free copy of my first book, *In the Footsteps of Greatness*. It is an award winning memoir about running the John Muir Trail in the Sierra Nevada wilderness of California (and who I had to become to get there). This book you're currently holding is an extension of that journey!

https://bit.ly/ITFOGFreeBook

Inspirational adventures are what I typically write about. If this is your bag please subscribe to my list below. No spam - just special content, fun stuff, random thoughts, and recommendations for other reads you might enjoy.

To your health and happiness!

www.joshmathe.com/mailing-list

CONTENTS

WHY?

I wrote this book for one reason: To clearly, effectively, and interactively help people develop more discipline (and by extension more fulfillment) in all the important aspects of their lives:

1. Spiritual/Service/Contribution
2. Physical/Nutrition/Health
3. Personal/Learning/Intellectual
4. Adventure/Lifestyle
5. Career/Business/Financial
6. Family/Friends/Relationships

The wheel below is a visual representation of these life areas.

My good friend Michael Nelson uses this same wheel in his outstanding book *Goals That Matter*, so you may have seen it before. There are other graphics like this and we can debate the details that should or should not be included, but I am confident this particular Wheel of Life accurately captures the broad categories that mean the most to us.

With that as our jumping off point, let us get started on this year of YOU...

INTRODUCTION

This is a book about discipline, but not discipline for discipline's sake. It is not some exercise in a vacuum designed to make you smile less, eat razor blades, and survive on no sleep. On the contrary, the goal of this book is to help you progressively add new skills to your quiver through applied, consistent effort. And to have fun doing it. You may be thinking "Wait, did he just imply that discipline can be fun?" Yes, yes I did. We're talking about the gamification of habit building baby! This is not your grandmother's "discipline".

I use the word *badass* in the subtitle, but I want to be clear - there are no axe throwing challenges in this book. What I am referring to is mastering the art of living as a complete, happy human. Comfortable in your own skin, authentic, real, and powerful. You will absolutely get an opportunity to push yourself physically over the next 365 days, but you will also be invited to grow mentally, spiritually, and emotionally.

This is also not a long book. It's not designed to give you an exhaustive review of the research and literature, and I will not spend 500 pages making my case. As Morgan Housel so eloquently points out in his fantastic book *The Psychology of Money,* "Most readers don't finish the books they begin because most single topics don't require 300 pages of explanation. I'd rather make 20 short points you finish than one long one you give up on". Amen. The science is out there, and I will give you resources for diving deeper into each area. In fact, I highly recommend doing this, because it's fun and interesting, and also because the more you understand something the easier it is to internalize it and make it your own. But, again, that's not my purpose here. I have worked with many clients over the years that lost themselves in books *about* doing rather than *actually* doing – as if somehow reading about something would bring it into their lives by osmosis. What I want to do here is give you just enough to spark your fire. This book is about action.

You will find as you progress, rather quickly I would imagine, that asking a little more of yourself and consciously stepping into challenge is actually intoxicatingly fun. As I write about in my book "*I, Athlete*", there is something alive in all of us that wants to be pushed and tested. I like to think of it as the primordial voice of our ancestors encouraging us. We are designed and evolved to do and be so much more than we currently are. Our bodies can run hundreds of miles to warn of an impending attack (look up the story of how the modern day marathon came to be). Our brains can learn to harness energy and build vehicles that propel us into space. Our spirits can love, and lose, and love again. We are incredible, otherworldly beings. All of us. Why not take yourself out for a test drive around the track of life and see just how many RPMs you can muster?

The premise is simple. Not easy. But supremely simple. I'm going to give you 12 challenges, one each month for a year. They will be progressive and build on one another in that every time you exercise your discipline muscle it gets stronger, but they will also stand alone. These challenges will address all the areas of our lives that are important for balance, health, and happiness. At the end of the year you will have 12 new habits, a powerful discipline ability, and be well on your way to one badass life.

Some of these challenges may be interesting experiences that teach you new skills but don't necessarily resonate. That's OK. Others may pluck your tuning fork in a way that rings forever because they noticeably add value and coalesce to make your life more awesome. Or you may experience something completely different. My advice is to let this process be organic.

You can go through this book in one shot, getting a feel for the challenges and what will be required before starting and then go back and complete them. Or, if you're like me and like to be surprised (no joke, you could hide my Christmas presents under my pillow and I wouldn't look) I encourage you to start with the first challenge and complete it before moving on. Choose your own adventure. With that said, my invitation (and challenge) at the outset is to simply commit. Right now. With no equivocation or stipulations. Don't do some of the challenges. Don't "make them your own". Don't make them easier or less uncomfortable. Just settle in, test your limits, and find out who you are.

Another note about the challenges: I have provided three
levels of difficulty/commitment for each. I have called these
Novice, Apprentice, and Master because I had to call them
something. But I title these with zero judgement. It is
purely about where you are in your journey. And you may
be at a different level in one challenge than you are in
another. That's OK! Pick the level that makes the most
sense for you on each challenge. Also, and I think this is
pretty cool – having three levels means that if you really
dive in and get turned on by this book, you could effectively
move through it three times over three years. Talk about life
changing! I just got full body skin tingles. Seriously. I love
this stuff and it's exciting to think about you falling in love
with it too.

My goal for you (and hopefully your goal for yourself) in
reading this book is not zenned out perfection. You're not
going to turn into the Dalai Lama. Sometimes, perhaps
much of the time, you won't be in the mood and will feel
like you're going through the motions. When you feel that
way remember that you're right where you need to be. Just
keep chopping wood and carrying water. Discipline (and
success in life) is about SHOWING UP. You will build
those muscles, you will make slow, unsexy progress, and you
will reach your goals and become who you want to become
by engaging in these daily habits consistently. Just
show up.

Finally, before jumping in I'd like to leave you with this: My
wife and I were watching American Idol last night, and in
the middle of the silly banter Lionel Richie dropped some
wisdom that made my hair stand on end. "Life begins at the

end of your comfort zone. The next time you are afraid, take a step forward". Word. Time to take that step forward.

CHALLENGE: BECOME A BIBLIOPHILE
PERSONAL/LEARNING/INTELLECTUAL

I am writing this at 6 AM after having woken up way too early on a Saturday. No reason, just couldn't sleep. But I'm not a crazy masochist. I didn't just leap out of bed and onto my computer. First, I made some killer coffee and sat down to read one of my favorite books. Early morning is a great time for this because the world hasn't woken up yet and nobody is requiring anything of you. Similarly, you often require less of yourself in these wee hours.

We all have a different relationship to reading. I was lucky enough to enjoy it immediately, getting lost in the adventures of Robin Hood and imagining myself fighting evil besides Garion (look this one up if you don't recognize it. One of the best fantasy series of all time). Others had trouble reading or weren't exposed to it and therefore have some negative associations with the written word. Yet others simply feel too busy or overwhelmed – or can't quiet their minds enough - to take the time and space to read. Whatever your personal relationship to reading, this month it is going to become robust!

Reading is so simple, yet exquisitely profound. A book can help you tap into shared wisdom or higher consciousness; it can teach you skills or offer new insights; it can be a friend in times of despair, or an escape when overwhelmed. Reading is a window into someone else's mind and soul so by its very nature it teaches us humility and empathy and broadens perspective. I would argue the simple act of choosing to take the time and space for yourself is also an important piece of claiming your life.

Practically speaking, engaging our brains, thinking and learning, keeps our brains young and growing. Literally. Your brain builds new pathways and neurons when you make it work, just like doing bicep curls. So, this month we are going to do some brain bicep curls – but with a comfortable chair and a hot mug of coffee instead of dumbbells...

NOVICE
Read for 15 minutes every day. The subject matter is your choice, but it must be a book (not a magazine, newspaper, blog, etc.) You can use an E reader or listen to the book on Audible if you must, but I would recommend participating in this challenge with an honest to goodness paper book. There is something gained from engaging with the experience in a more tactile way. The sandy feeling of the book pages on your fingers. The crisp flip of the pages. Even the smell of the ink and paper. It is immersive in a way the other mediums aren't.

APPRENTICE
Read for 30 minutes every day. Same rules as above in that the subject matter is your choice but it must be a book and I highly recommend making it a *paper* book. And to turn up

the juice on the challenge, keep a notecard for each book and add to it as you read. What words don't you know? What questions spark your interest? What destinations warrant some research? Keep a running inventory of anything that bubbles up for you while you're reading, and then when you've finished the book write down three key takeaways AND how they can add value to your life.

MASTER

Read for at least 60 minutes a day AND finish a book a week. I read for an hour a day most of the time but almost never in one sitting. Break this up into as many sessions as you need. I realize an hour a day may feel like a lot, but it simply comes down to priorities. You can watch TV, play XBox, plant a garden, or read with your "free" time. But if you're a master reader, I don't have to tell you that!

Like the challenges above I'd like you to read books only. Also, as a master, your goal is to have two books going at a time – one for pleasure, and one for intellectual advancement (business, spirituality, etc.). Please make at least one of these an actual paper book, but feel free to make the other a digital or audio book. Keep a notecard for each book and engage with the material as described above. Using this strategy, you will be able to knock out more books in a year than you ever thought possible! My personal best is 96 books in a calendar year. Email me and let me know if you beat me and I'll send you a prize!

WORDS OF WISDOM FROM THE BEST...
(*Every month I will leave you with some food for thought from a subject matter expert*)

Ryan Holiday, best-selling author and the most prolific reader I have ever seen, bluntly asserts "There's a reason it was illegal to teach slaves to read. There is a reason that every totalitarian regime has burned and banned books. Knowledge is power."

He also has some great advice about how to fit reading (or more reading) into your already busy life:
Read first thing in the morning
Read a page a day
Read while you eat
Read while you relax
Change your story about being busy. You are not too busy to prioritize what's important.

These are simple yet actionable suggestions, and I love them because they work – and they will work for many of the other challenges in this book as well. Use the small spaces in between things, and BE someone who efficiently and effectively embraces success habits (vs whatever story you are telling yourself now).

RECOMMENDED READING
(I am also going to give you a handful of book suggestions to further your understanding or enjoyment of that particular subject. Some of the these recommendations will clearly link to the challenge, and others will be a bit more like Daniel-san painting fences to learn karate)

Patterson, Kerry, et al. *Change Anything: The New Science of Personal Success.* Grand Central Publishing, 2011.

Adler, Mortimer J., et al. *How To Read a Book: The Classic Guide to Intelligent Reading.* Touchstone, 2011.

Hardy, Darren. *The Compound Effect: Jumpstart Your Income, Your Life, Your Success.* Hachette Go, 10th Anniversary Edition, 2020.

CHALLENGE 1 - REFLECTIONS

Please take a few minutes to think about the past 30 days and answer these questions. Write them down someplace where you can come back and revisit your thoughts. A nice journal is a great place for this.

What were the key takeaways from this month?

What (if anything) do I plan to incorporate into my life moving forward?

Has my relationship with reading changed?

MONTH 2

CHALLENGE: CHANNEL GRATITUDE
SPIRITUAL/SERVICE/CONTRIBUTION

An attitude of gratitude. Very simple but perhaps the single most monumentally high payoff activity in this book. All of these challenges are about building new brain wiring, so it's important to point out that two states can't exist at the same time in your brain. If you are thinking about what you are grateful for there is no room for any negativity. Just doesn't work. Grateful thoughts and feelings literally and measurably change your mental and emotional experience and attract more positive thoughts and emotions. Engaging in this exercise regularly builds an ever-deepening habit groove that allows you to exist in this state for longer periods of time. Until it is simply your norm. Happy, hopeful, positive, calm. So in a very real way this challenge is preparing your mental garden for the flowers and vegetables you will be planting in later chapters.

I mention gratitude in my other books because it is such a powerful tool for a happier, more connected mindset. However, in those books I give broad suggestions and let you choose how to accomplish it. Here, I'm going to tell you exactly what to do (at least for the challenge).

Also, remember that this stuff is cumulative. You've probably dabbled with gratitude journals before, or even tried to sit in that headspace for a few minutes at a time. That's fantastic. But by engaging in gratitude daily, consciously, and consistently we are going to profoundly reshape your internal (and mostly likely by extension external) landscape.

NOVICE
Keep a daily gratitude journal. Write down 5 things you are grateful for in that moment. An effective way to incorporate this journal is to do it at the end of the day and note things that happened during that day you are grateful for. There are no rules here. You can be grateful for people, places, events, relationships, weather, etc. Some of the smallest things can be the most poignant. The smell of coffee and warmth of the sunshine show up in my gratitude on many occasions. If you have a meditation/silence/prayer practice I encourage you to pair this exercise with it.

APPRENTICE
Keep a daily gratitude journal (see above) AND wake up with gratitude. As soon as you wake up, before reaching for your phone or going over your mental checklist of tasks you need to accomplish, just lay there and breathe. Think about what you are grateful for in that moment. Your relationship with loved ones often fits well here, but again there are no rules. Just be with your gratitude and ride its unique wave each morning. It may quietly ebb or crash with a thun-

derous boom. It may last for a few seconds or luxuriously stretch for minutes.

Master

Complete both Novice and Apprentice exercises (keep a gratitude journal and wake up with gratitude) AND tell someone every day how much you appreciate them. This can be accomplished using any medium you prefer. In person is wonderful, but phone, text, video chat, or email are all acceptable. The important thing is that your sentiments are authentic and heartfelt. I like to think of this as "finding the gold" in people. Almost everyone has some aspects of their personalities that are challenging for us - and these are the things we tend to focus on. But these same people all have unique and admirable qualities as well. Sometimes the same flaws that annoy us are the quirks we enjoy, and the only thing different is our perspective (you will find that the more you practice gratitude, the more you automatically see the gold).

Remember, this doesn't have to be weird or forced. Just real.

"Hey man. Thanks for your help on the proposal yesterday. It was great to have support."

"Just wanted to let you know I appreciate you listening yesterday. I really needed it."

"You're awesome! The front yard looks so good!"

Words of wisdom from the best...

Of course I'm going to give you some Dalai Llama goodness here. I don't know if you've ever read anything he's written or listened to him speak, but he is an incredible human being. Here are a couple of his thoughts about gratitude.

"Everyday, think as you wake up: Today I am fortunate to have woken up. I am alive. I have a precious human life. I am not going to waste it. I am going to use all my energies to develop myself, to expand my heart out to others, to achieve enlightenment for the benefit of all beings. I am going to have kind thoughts towards others, I am not going to get angry, or think badly about others. I am going to benefit others as much as I can."

Also, something I think many of us achievers could stand to internalize: "When you are discontent, you always want more, more, more. Your desire can never be satisfied. But when you practice contentment, you can say to yourself, 'Oh yes – I already have everything that I really need."

This is so beautiful in its simple truth. Gratitude, contentment, thankfulness-they are all the same. Discontent occurs when there is a gap between where we are and where we want to be. Our great opportunity in life is to authentically appreciate the place we currently stand while looking with excitement toward where we are going.

Recommended Reading
Lama, Dalai, et al. *The Book of Joy: Lasting Happiness in a Changing World*. Avery, 2016.

Hesse Herman. *Siddhartha*. Countless publications and editions but originally published in Germany in 1922 and then New Directions published it in the United States in 1951.

Kaplan, Janice. *The Gratitude Diaries: How a Year Looking on the Bright Side Can Transform Your Life*. Dutton, 2015.

CHALLENGE 2 - REFLECTIONS

Please take a few minutes to think about the past 30 days and answer these questions. Write them down someplace where you can come back and revisit your thoughts.

What were the key takeaways from this month?

What (if anything) do I plan to incorporate into my life moving forward?

Are there people or situations in my life that I could feel better about simply by focusing a floodlight of gratitude in their direction?

MONTH 3

CHALLENGE: DAILY ADVENTURE
ADVENTURE/LIFESTYLE

Confession: I wrote these challenges in the order by which they excited me the most and this one was right at the top. I strongly believe that life is meant to be lived. I like to think of it as a grand buffet just waiting to be sampled and it's my job – dang, it it's my duty – to sample as much of that buffet as I can before my time is up. I don't want to leave any juice in the orange! And I don't want you to either.

Sadly, this is an area of our lives that is often overlooked. In modern, overachieving society it is engrained in us to charge hard, to buckle down, and to spend serious time on serious things. These principles have their rightful place in a balanced life and certainly lead to prosperity and trophies. However, they don't necessarily contribute to happiness or fulfillment. Enter adventure.

I don't care who you are or how buttoned up you've become; I know a tingle runs up your spine when you crest a hill and look across the horizon or when your bare feet touch the warm sand of a hidden beach. It's just how we are wired. We are here to explore, and adventure feeds our bodies and souls just like water and sunlight. If you are already tapped into this reservoir of deliciousness, fantastic. This will be a fun month for you. If not, hallelujah – this will be a fun and really important month for you! Here is your challenge:

Novice

Explore somewhere new every day. Adventure doesn't have to come in the form of exotic sand dunes or a tangled, rainforest labyrinth. It can be found every day, in every nook and cranny of your normal life. Sure, it takes you actually exploring some new places but it's also about your mindset. Set your mental compass to look for wonder and to notice magic. Does this sound crazy? Maybe a bit. But it's also a truly fun way to approach your life.

So, at least once a day for this entire month consciously extricate yourself from the busy routine of your life and go on walkabout. Check out a new bike path in your neighborhood. Sit and take in the scene at the local brewery you keep hearing about. Climb to the top of that hill you always look at but never really see. It doesn't have to take hours or even take you out of your city. Heck, as long as you approach this with an open heart and eyes, go for a walk around the block. BUT – choose a different path AND really see things. Put the phone down and notice the colors of the rocks, the dew on the leaves, the piercing shriek of the hawk circling above you. Take in the world with newborn eyes. To a baby, everything is an adventure! And this freshness is like a bath for your spirit.

Apprentice

Explore somewhere new everyday PLUS twice during the month go on a road trip to somewhere you have never visited. Same challenge as the Novice but you get to add road trips. Twice this month get out of dodge. And remember that the adventure begins with the first spark of the idea. Get excited and enjoy the planning process. The only requirement is that you have to journey to a new destination. And while you're there practice all the same magic noticing that you do on a daily basis! Chat with locals, take off your shoes, wander through a farmer's market sampling produce. Make it as tactile and present as possible.

Master

Explore somewhere new everyday PLUS twice during the month go on a road trip to somewhere you have never visited AND make one of those trips a bucket list destination that is at least 1000 miles away. Same as both above, but you get the delightful pleasure of exploring a once in a lifetime destination (although I hate it when people say "once in a lifetime". The reality is that if you plan your life right there is no reason you can't visit the Taj Mahal five times. So, strike that. Let's call it a fantastically life affirming destination instead !)

I realize this takes money, planning, and schedule freedom. That's why it is in the Master category. Nobody said this would be easy or comfortable. Presumably you're reading this book because you are drawn to the idea of living the fullest expression of your life? To living completely and audaciously out loud? To making your own decisions about what is important and fulfilling and what isn't? Well, I can't speak for you but enjoying a glass of wine and caprese salad in the shadow of the

Duomo sure fills this niche for me. What about you?
Where have you always wanted to go? What has stopped
you up to this point? If you have a legitimate reason (for
instance, I am not suggesting you go into debt or sell a
child so that you can see the Eifel tower for the first time)
then stick to the Novice or Apprentice offerings in the
challenge and make Master an exciting goal to work
toward. However, if your family, job, and bank account
will survive without you for a couple weeks – bon
voyage!

Similar to the advice above, don't just travel there. BE
there. Soak it in. Try locale fare that scares you with its
abundant eyes and tentacles. Attempt to speak the
language. Move by horse, or elephant, or dirt bike for the
first time. If you're lucky enough to be someone who
already travels frequently, what can you do to take it up a
notch? Join a science boat doing research at the Marianas
trench? Perhaps trek to Mecca? Buddy up to Elon Musk
and find yourself orbiting the Earth? There is actually a
multi-day adventure race in the jungles of Costa Rica that
requires you to undergo special forces training before
participating!

* You can combine this with another challenge like the Big
Rock coming up later. You can also put the Master chal-
lenge at another time later in the year if that works better.
Just make it happen!

WORDS OF WISDOM FROM THE BEST...
When it comes to adventure, I can't think of anyone who
embodied this spirit more than the great John Muir. He was
a renowned writer, naturalist, philosopher, botanist, glaciol-

ogist, and political activist that oozed adventure from every pore of his body.

Muir once said "I only went out for a walk, and finally concluded to stay out till sundown, for going out, I found, was really going in." He added, "Few places in this world are more dangerous than home. Fear not, therefore, to try the mountain passes. They will kill care, save you from deadly apathy, set you free, and call forth every faculty into vigorous, enthusiastic action."

RECOMMENDED READING

Guillebeau, Chris. *The Happiness of Pursuit: Finding the Quest that Will Bring Purpose to Your Life* . Harmony, 2014.

Stillman, Scott. *Wilderness, The Gateway to the Soul: Spiritual Enlightenment Through Wilderness*. Wild Soul Press, 2018.

Roberts, Gregory David. *Shantaram: A Novel*. St. Martin's Press, 2004.

Bryson, Bill. *A Walk in the Woods: Rediscovering America on the Appalachian Trail*. Crown, 2010.

CHALLENGE 3 - REFLECTIONS

Please take a few minutes to think about the past 30 days and answer these questions. Write them down someplace where you can come back and revisit your thoughts.

What were the key takeaways from this month?

What (if anything) do I plan to incorporate into my life moving forward?

Do I allow myself to get excited about something everyday?

CHALLENGE: KICK THE JUICE
PHYSICAL/NUTRITION/HEALTH

Now you're going to hate me. Just for a bit, until you've come through the other side to green pastures filled with unicorns. For this challenge you're going to give up some "foods" that your body (and brain) have really grown to rely on. Which means it may be tough. Good. There is power in that crucible.

Given what we currently know about food and the body, processed foods and sugar are the single biggest causes of inflammation and disease. And they are insidiously addictive. This is why they are so hard to forgo. When you gobble down a brownie, I'm pretty sure you already know that you are ingesting a few hundred calories of empty calories and inflaming your body with substances that it barely recognizes as food. But perhaps even more disturbing is the fact that the constant chemical and sugar drip to your brain is making you want even more, and more often.

Is the goal of this challenge to force you to give up "bad" food for the rest of your life? Not necessarily. (By the way, I don't like to characterize food as "good" or "bad" – there are simply foods that take you closer to your goals, and others that carry you farther away) I recognize how challenging and upriver that would be in today's world. What I do want for you is to break the chemical and emotional dependence on foods that have a hold on you, to learn new habits, and to prove to yourself you can do it. What we are doing here is fundamentally changing your relationship with food so that you have choice and can make conscious, thoughtful decisions about what and when you eat. So that you have power over your food instead of the other way around.

NOVICE

No sugar. What I mean by that is: No foods that have sugar added to them. No sugar substitutes or artificial sweeteners (sugar substitutes like stevia, monk fruit, or sugar alcohols like Erythritol don't have the same caloric impact as "regular" sugar, but it looks like our bodies still interpret them as sugar, and they definitely still keep us craving sweetness). No honey. And be on the lookout for all the names and faces sugar hides as: glucose, fructose, high fructose corn syrup, brown rice syrup, molasses, sucrose, dextrose, etc. This does not include fruit. You can have *1-2 pieces* of fruit a day. Yes, fruit has sugar in it (added by nature, not humans) but it also contains nutrients and fiber so I call it a wash. For this same reason you can eat complex carbohydrates like vegetables, brown rice or hearty, brown bread (as long as there has been no sugar added). I once heard a doctor ask the question, "Has anyone ever become obese because of their apple habit?" Touché.

This may be challenging for the first few days as your body comes off the sugar high. You may get a bit grumpy, and you will almost assuredly crave some sugary things. But you can do it! Settle in and try to enjoy the fact that your body is changing in extremely health promoting ways. I promise it quickly gets easier and your cravings and tastebuds actually change. When carrots start tasting like candy you have arrived at the promised land! And no, I am not exaggerating.

Am I expecting you to never have sugar for the rest of your life? No. But I do want you to internalize the fact that you don't need it and experience what it feels like to live without it.

Apprentice

No sugar OR processed food, period. What I am defining as processed food for this challenge is: Anything that wasn't grown, picked, killed, or handmade. Anything bagged or boxed. Anything with an ingredients list more than a few items long that includes terms you don't recognize and can't pronounce (and probably anything with an ingredients list period). Anything with preservatives, additives, chemicals, etc. Canned and frozen food is OK as long as nothing was added to it. Bread, rice, pasta, baked goods, candy, soda, salad dressing, and most dairy products are all no go's. If you can find whole, organic dairy products (goat derivations are particularly good because goat's milk is more nutritious, hypoallergenic, and may increase nutrient absorption) that is acceptable in minimal quantities. I know dairy is composed of sugar. Like fruit, if you consume it in small amounts and choose high quality products I would consider it a net neutral to your body. That is simply my opinion – but since it's my book and my challenge, those are the rules.

If reducing dairy sounds scary (fun, that rhymes) I get it. I was raised in the 80's during the heyday of the dairy industry's meteoric rise; a result of one of the most massive and effective marketing campaign's of all time. Our nubile brains were no match for the iconic tagline "Milk, it does a body good" or the superstar athlete gracing the pages of our favorite magazines with glistening abs and a milk mustache.

The reality is that we are the only species that drinks another species' milk, and that consuming significant quantities of dairy is strongly linked to inflammation and disease. We absolutely don't need dairy to receive all of our essential nutrients. All the things you associate with dairy - calcium, protein, phosphorous - are all found in other foods in abundance. Focusing on fruits, vegetables, nuts, seeds, and whole grains with a light sprinkling of high quality meat, fish, and/or dairy will top off your nutrient stores just fine.

Part 2 of the challenge is to take a moment before eating (every time) and ask yourself "Why am I eating right now?" And then really listen to the answer. Are you hungry? Tired? Bored? Sad? There are a multitude of reasons we eat, and only one is to nourish our bodies. You should find this a very enlightening experience and it will start bringing a whole new level of awareness to your food decisions.

MASTER

Complete the full 2-part Apprentice challenge PLUS you are going completely plant based this month. No animal products of any kind. Based on everything we know about longevity, disease, and general wellbeing a plant-based diet is a worthy goal.

I realize this might sound ludicrous if you are someone that is comforted by meat and potatoes, but I encourage you to give it a try with an open mind and curious taste buds. You may be surprised how much you love eating this way. Flavors come alive on an entirely different spectrum. And, bear with me here, there is something intangibly... satisfying about eating food that purely and truly nourishes you. My sister and I were at a silent retreat the first time I felt this inscrutable connection to my food and it was profound. We only received two meals per day, but they were prepared with great care and entirely made from ingredients grown in the organic garden on the property. I can't even describe how gratifying those meals were, and they could not have been simpler. But my body responded to the whole, real fruits, vegetables, and grains in a way it never had before. If you have ever experienced what I'm talking about you're vigorously nodding your head right now – and if you haven't, get ready to be surprised!

Of course, if you've never cooked this way there is a bit of a learning curve. Enjoy that too. Hopefully when the challenge is over you will have learned some new techniques and preparations and discovered a whole host of new foods to incorporate and relish. If you'd like some guidance, I have included two links below. You are also welcome to email me for help and I will gladly don my nutritionist hat to put something together for you.

https://www.veganeasy.org/30-day-challenge/30-day-menu/

https://www.forksoverknives.com/meal-planner/

If you'd like to eat this way but just want the food delivered to your door, there are great companies like Purple Carrot that have you covered; either with pre-made meals or ingredients that you can put together yourself.

WORDS OF WISDOM FROM THE BEST...

Mark Bittman is a brilliant food journalist, author, and former columnist for the New York Times who has dedicated his life to improving the way humans eat. According to Bittman, "The evidence is overwhelming at this point. You eat more plants, you eat less other stuff, you live longer. 50-100 years from now we are all going to be eating a plant-based diet. Whether that happens through catastrophe or a peaceful, sustainable, life giving way is based on whether we make the right choices now and how we fight in this struggle together".

Another of Bittman's insights made me sit up and widen my eyes when I read it. "Junk food companies are acting very much like tobacco companies did 30 years ago".

It is simply no longer acceptable to shrug our shoulders, look the other way, and continue to stuff our faces with Pop Tarts and Oreos. We need to be better than this. YOU need to be better than this. Stop eating food that isn't food.

RECOMMENDED READING

Campbell, Colin T. *The China Study: The Most Comprehensive Study of Nutrition Ever Conducted and the Startling Implications for Diet, Weight Loss, and Long-Term Health.* BenBella Books, Revised Edition, 2016.

Brazier, Brendan. *Thrive: The Plant-Based Whole Foods*

Way to Staying Healthy for Life. Da Capo Lifelong Books, 10th Anniversary Edition, 2017.

Bittman, Mark. *Animal, Vegetable, Junk: A History of Food from Sustainable to Suicidal*. Mariner Books, 2021.

Greger, Michael MD, et al. *How Not to Die: Discover the Foods Scientifically Proven to Prevent and Reverse Disease*. Flatiron Books, 2015.

Any of Michael Pollan's books

CHALLENGE 4 - REFLECTIONS

Please take a few minutes to think about the past 30 days and answer these questions. Write them down someplace where you can come back and revisit your thoughts.

What were the key takeaways from this month?

What (if anything) do I plan to incorporate into my life moving forward?

What physical changes did I notice in my body this month?

MONTH 5

CHALLENGE: CONNECT
FAMILY/FRIENDS/RELATIONSHIPS

I remember one Thanksgiving years ago... we were all sitting around my parent's dining room table, loaded plates teeming with all manner of gluttonous splendor. As is the custom, one of my parents expressed gratitude for family and for all of us coming together. I think it was my mom. At one point she used the word "connection" in reference to what we were doing. What we were creating. And one of my dad's brothers wrinkled his forehead and interrupted her.

"Connection? What does that mean?" He said, genuinely perplexed.

It should be noted, he was a hard-charging, ultra-successful (financially), achievement oriented, stockbroker at the time. Probably not unlike many of you reading this book. Hopefully at this point in time and our place in history you know what I mean when I say "connection". But just in case, I would characterize connection as that ungraspable but very tangible energy between us and all things around us. That little thrill that runs through you when you meet someone new and discover that you both played the same sport in high school or read and love the same obscure author. The warmth that blooms in your midsection when a puppy wriggles on your lap. The sense of vast oneness that envelopes you when you stand on a mountain looking down at the azure lake below. And a thousand other examples. You know what I mean.

For all of us, regardless of how independent or cynical we are, connection is imperative for health and certainly happiness. In *The Blue Zones*, Dan Buettner talks about the 9 factors that lead to longevity. Not surprisingly, connection is at the top of the list. Of course, there are different kinds of connection. Connection to a higher power, connection to your life's purpose, or connection to nature for instance. These are great and I encourage you to explore them. For this challenge we are going to nurture our connection with other people – which I would argue may be the most important connection of all.

Some of us recognize how much we need and yearn for connection. Others aren't as self-aware (and to be fair, we all experience this differently). Either way, few of us actively foster connection in our lives. So that's what we're going to do this month. If this feels too touchy feely for you, I get it. There was a time in my life when I would have rolled my eyes at this challenge too. The hard to quantify nature of connection would have frustrated me. If this describes you, try approaching the challenge from an entirely pragmatic perspective. When you feel connected to people that you care about, it stimulates the release of hormones that fight disease, and causes you to feel happier and more peaceful.

This in turn helps you live a longer, more productive life. If you are motivated to be the best version of yourself and to conquer as many goals as possible, connection is a major foundational piece. Of course, if you're motivated to just experience the simple joy of life and feel good, connection kicks ass in this regard too!

For all levels of challenge, don't worry about *measuring* connection. Just focus on the daily tasks and let the connection take care of itself.

NOVICE

Text one friend or family member every day. The subject matter isn't important. It's great if you choose to say something inherently connecting like "Hey Mom! I was just thinking about how much I love you!" but it's not necessary to be that blatant. Just the act of reaching out and then them reaching back creates the spark or fans a flame that is already burning. Say what's in your heart at the moment, let them know you're thinking about them (again, just the act of reaching out will serve that purpose), and let it be what it is. It may develop into a conversation or it may just be a quick virtual high five.

APPRENTICE

Text one friend or family member every day (see above) AND hand write a card and mail it each day. Yes, I'm serious. Like with paper and ink. If you are under 30 ask an older friend to explain it. These cards can go to anyone. Friends, family, co-workers, new business relationships, etc. A thank you is always a good reason to reach out, but the subject matter is up to you.

This simple act has profound results. Because handwritten cards are so rare nowadays, the impact of receiving one is magnified. Think about the last time you received a handwritten note, particularly if it was unexpected (not a birthday). Weren't you touched and impressed that someone would take the time and energy to make you feel special? Also, a little added bonus is that the writer (you in this case) receives a jolt of karmic goodness. It's like giving a little Christmas gift every day. So, you get to feel yummy for writing it, and they get to feel yummy for receiving it. A connection explosion.

MASTER

Complete the same tasks as the two challenges above AND once a week complete a video or in person chat with someone special in your life with the intent to listen deeply and have them feel heard. Open your ears, close your mouth, and truly hear the person across from you. Practice listening with the intent not to respond, but to "get" the other person, wherever they may be in that moment. When a response feels appropriate, make it a reflection and check in to make sure you understood them - DO NOT give advice, tell a story about yourself, or a make a joke to deflect strong emotion. (Please note - this interaction must be with someone you care about. Work calls don't count, unless you really care about the co-worker and consider them a good friend outside of work)

This trifecta of a text, handwritten card, and voice/face interaction on a daily basis is a potent brew of connection. I realize it takes some significant planning and energy expenditure to coordinate and follow through with this for a month. That's why it's the master challenge. I also realize a phone call or video chat might sound like chewing glass to some of you. I'm actually right there with you. As extroverted as I often appear, I recharge my batteries alone in the woods. And while I enjoy people it absolutely takes energy to interact with them, even if they are my favorite people. So, I completely understand how hard this challenge might be. I also know that it's entirely achievable and that cultivating connection in this manner is worth the potential discomfort and energy expenditure.

WORDS OF WISDOM FROM THE BEST...

Dr. Brené Brown is amazing. A PhD and MSW, Dr. Brown is a research professor at the University of Houston that has spent the last two decades studying vulnerability, shame, empathy and courage. She has also written five NY Times bestselling books and hosts two wildly popular podcasts. If anyone understands the power of connection, it's her.

"I define connection as the energy that exists between people when they feel seen, heard, and valued; when they can give and receive without judgment; and when they derive sustenance and strength from the relationship. Connection is why we're here. We are hardwired to connect with others, it's what gives purpose and meaning to our lives, and without it there is suffering."

Enough said.

RECOMMENDED READING

Brown, Brené. *Daring Greatly: How the Courage to Be Vulnerable Transforms the Way We Live, Love, Parent, and Lead.* Avery, 2012.

Buettner, Dan. The Blue Zones: 9 Lessons for Living Longer From the People Who've Lived the Longest. National Geographic, 2nd Edition, 2012.

Frankl, Viktor. *Man's Search for Meaning.* Originally published in Vienna in 1946 and has sold over 9 million copies worldwide.

CHALLENGE 5 - REFLECTIONS

Please take a few minutes to think about the past 30 days and answer these questions. Write them down someplace where you can come back and revisit your thoughts.

What were the key takeaways from this month?

What (if anything) do I plan to incorporate into my life moving forward?

How would I define connection and how do I know when I feel connected to someone?

MONTH 6

CHALLENGE: PAY YOURSELF FIRST

CAREER/BUSINESS/FINANCIAL

If you're anything like me, just thinking about money makes you break out in hives. I used to have a whole host of negative core beliefs about money and strange judgements and insecurities around my relationship to it. I even had the common but ridiculous deep-seated belief that money was bad and that people with money were bad, and that being wealthy was something to be ashamed of. Of course, nothing could be further from the truth. I have spent much of my adult life rewiring these beliefs and finding a healthier and more accurate mindset around money. The reality is that good people do good things with money, bad people do bad things with money, and money itself is inherently neutral. And there is no denying that having more money helps you lead the life you want to lead – especially if that includes doing great things with it.

The real key for me was to start thinking about my financial health and goals as WEALTH rather than money. Because wealth encompasses everything that's important to me: purpose, passion, joy, fun, adventure, helping people, travel, security, connection, a lake house, cool new electric cars, etc. Basically, the entire Quan from Jerry Maguire. Money facilitates all of this – and that stokes my fire big time. So, the important thing is to connect to something about your financial health that lights you up and to dive into that with both feet.

The interesting thing about your finances is that they are really simple. Like losing weight. If you consume less calories than you expend you will lose weight. Boom. Insanely simple. But not easy. Because we all have those weird stories and wonky brain wiring that I just referred to. Especially around money. Being financially healthy is also simple. Spend less than you make. Spend on what is important to you and not on what isn't. Save. Know where your money is going. Do things to help your money grow while you sleep. Generosity boomerangs back to the source. This isn't a financial book, but a healthy relationship with money is an important piece of your life success, and my goal is to help you either start building some discipline in this area, or double down on the discipline you've already developed.

Novice
Conduct an audit of your expenses. Look at the last 6 months to a year. Where does your money go? Identify one key area of waste and channel that into savings. Your goal is a $1000 liquid emergency fund. Start saving 5% of your income, right off the top before you do anything else with it to achieve this goal.

Knowing that 5% number, work backward and set a DAILY automatic transfer from your checking to your savings account. Or, if you want to emotionally engage with this process more you can actually put cash in a jar. Either way, do it daily and without fail. We are building the saving/delayed gratification muscle. Most of the world is terrible at this and this is your opportunity to set yourself apart.

APPRENTICE

Your goal is similar to the Novice level, but we are going to turn up the knob a bit. <u>Conduct your expense audit, identify one or two key areas of waste, and begin setting aside 10% of your income, right off the top before you do *anything* else with it.</u>

If you already have $1000 liquid emergency fund, create a plan for your debt and begin attacking this with a vengeance. List all your debt (not including your house or student loans - these are both long term investments in self and are generally bigger numbers and lower interest rates), how much you owe, what the minimum payments are, and what interest rate you are paying on each. Financially it probably makes slightly more sense to pay off the biggest debts first, but emotionally I am a big fan of Dave Ramsey's snowball approach where you target your smallest debts first. It just feels good to see success quickly.

If 10% is the most you can manage toward servicing your debt, great. If you can throw even more than 10% at it, go for it! Make the minimum payment on all loans except the smallest one - throw everything else at that until it's gone. Rinse and repeat. And imagine how good it will feel (and how much more freedom of choice you will have) once you don't have debt sitting on your shoulders.

MASTER

If you are ready to take on the challenges in this category, congratulations! You clearly have some mad money skills. And you may know most or all of this already and be in a solid place. But let's find your opportunity area!

You already have a basic $1000 liquid emergency fund. Your debt and its pay-off is either complete or close to it (other than your house and/or student loans, which are longer pay-off assets). Now you are going to focus on real wealth building and lifestyle creation. If you haven't already done an expense audit or haven't completed one in a while, do so. Identify all areas of waste or possibility. Do your expenses match your priorities? Begin saving at least 15% of your income, right off the top before doing *anything* else with it – with the goal of accumulating an amount equal to 3-6 months of your living expenses.

Once you have that cushion, and you are a master at what you need to spend money on and what you can do without, focus on continuing to save that 15%, and now begin to invest it. And we are talking 15% of your gross income. Talk to a financial advisor about the best place to put this money but it doesn't have to be fancy. Probably just a retirement account like a ROTH. The key is consistency. The goal is to gradually accumulate a nest egg that supports you and allows you to live an incredible life on 8% of it. Why 8%? It should be enough to hedge inflation and live very comfortably while still allowing your money to grow. Once you are shoveling 15% into your retirement accounts, then you can put a full court press on paying off your mortgage and/or student loans with whatever you have leftover.

Once all of your debt is paid off and you are truly, completely debt free you have reached some rarified air. This is when you can start focusing on some really cool stuff. Have even more fun (you should be doing this all along FYI). Give to people and organizations that touch your heart in ways that truly affect change. One of my best friends actually has a "Giving Account" where he puts a significant portion of his income simply so that he can do more things for other people. At this point in your life and financial journey you have probably already internalized the basic law of the universe that the secret to happiness and fulfillment is to be of service. So, dive into that and splash around! I also highly recommend reading the books *Abundance* and *Bold* by pioneer futurist Peter Diamandis. Both books take a broad look at the science and people at the forefront of humanity's exciting future and how you can get involved.

* There is a bunch of specific advice in this chapter gleaned from a host of experts. Granted, that's true for every chapter, but we tend to have very strong emotions about our money. So you may be uncomfortable right now. That's OK. Regardless of how you feel about my suggestions, please focus on the nugget I am attempting to polish. Pay yourself first. Whether it's 5% or 15%, whether you choose to pay down your mortgage or not, be strategic. Wealth isn't about how much you make, it is about how much you keep.

WORDS OF WISDOM FROM THE BEST...
"In the end, managing your finances well is a lot like developing a strong personal productivity system: You keep track of everything without making it your full-time job; you set goals; you break them down into small bite-size

tasks; you save yourself time by automating manual work; and you spend your time and brainpower focusing on the big picture. That's what I try to do with my time and money."

"Conscious spending isn't about cutting your spending on everything. That approach wouldn't last two days. It is, quite simply, about choosing the things you love enough to spend extravagantly on—and then cutting costs mercilessly on the things you don't love."

These pearls are brought to you by Ramit Sethi – creative financial thinker, New York Times bestselling author, and founder of I Will Teach You To Be Rich. There are countless personal finance gurus who are all clamoring to grab your attention – and all with their own strategies and advice. I like Ramit because his approach is easy, intuitive, and common sense. And he doesn't shy away from hard truths.

RECOMMENDED READING
Ramsey, Dave. *The Total Money Makeover: A Proven Plan for Financial Fitness*. Thomas Nelson, 2013.

Sethi, Ramit. *I Will Teach You to Be Rich: No Guilt. No Excuses. No BS. Just a 6-Week Program That Works*. Workman Publishing Company, Revised Edition, 2019.

Michalowicz, Mike. *Profit First: Transform Your Business from a Cash-Eating Monster to a Money-Making Machine*. Portfolio, Reissue Edition, 2017.

Housel, Morgan. *The Psychology of Money: Timeless*

Lessons on Wealth, Greed, and Happiness. Harriman House, 2020.

Diamandis, Peter H, et al. *Abundance: The Future is Better Than You Think*. Free Press, Reprint Edition, 2012.

Diamandis, Peter H, et al. *Bold: How to Go Big, Create Wealth, and Impact the World*. Simon & Schuster, Reprint Edition, 2015.

CHALLENGE 6 - REFLECTIONS

Please take a few minutes to think about the past 30 days and answer these questions. Write them down someplace where you can come back and revisit your thoughts.

What were the key takeaways from this month?

What (if anything) do I plan to incorporate into my life moving forward?

Do I have any negative core beliefs about money that fundamentally aren't true?

CHALLENGE: LEARN EVERYDAY
PERSONAL/LEARNING/INTELLECTUAL

Caveat – I'm a big dork. With that said, this challenge rocks! Permission to take time out of your day to engage your brain and learn something new? Yes please. At this point I probably don't have to convince you how important it is to challenge your brain regularly and to push it to new and uncomfortable places. The science is ubiquitous and well documented. It is simply a fact that learning new things keeps our brains younger, healthier, and working properly. And did I mention how fun it is?

We have all heard that it gets harder to learn new things as we get older. And it may be true that we as we age, we don't form new brain cells to replace old ones quite as fast as we used to. But if you are buying into an "old dogs can't learn new tricks" or "demise is inevitable" narrative, that's just balderdash (bet you didn't think I could sneak that word into a book). Aging is inevitable. Decay is a choice. I don't care if you are 15 or 95, your brain is capable of learning new things and building fresh neurons.

The other important piece of this challenge is that you must be learning entirely *new* things. If you have a job or a hobby that requires you to learn new skills and processes, that's great – but this is about pushing yourself into unfamiliar, thorny places and engaging virgin parts of your brain that have been lying dormant. Get wild with this one.

NOVICE

Pick a subject that you have always wanted to know more about. Spend 15 minutes a day learning about it and 30 days becoming a subject matter expert (as much as possible. If you're trying your hand at physics, I don't expect you to become Albert Einstein in four weeks). I also don't want this to become a job. If you feel like you've learned enough to satisfy your curiosity, go ahead and move on to another area of interest. But please check in with yourself before doing this and make sure you aren't suffering from shiny object syndrome. In today's world we are SO accustomed to having multiple things operating at any one time and staying as shallow as possible – and our brains have built those patterns. You may have noticed that it's harder to focus or think deeply than it used to be. That's not because you're old. It's because the world we now live in teaches our brains to scatter and splat. Consciously choose not to do that during this challenge.

You can complete your learning through reading, talking to people, internet searches, watching videos, etc. - the more the merrier. You may even purposely choose many modes of ingestion to see what feels right and what stretches your brain.

If you are interested in some formal and organized guidance, I highly recommend checking out websites like MasterClass and One Day University. There is incredible learning to be had on these sites from some of the world's best educators and experts. I just finished a Master-Class about negotiation from former FBI hostage negotiator Chris Voss that was mind blowingly interesting. You can also sign up for a traditional class at a college in your area or online.

Apprentice

For the Apprentice challenge you are going to get more hands on and spend more time. Your goal is to dedicate at least 30 minutes a day to learning a new language, musical instrument, or sport. All three of these require massive brain engagement, and two of them have the added benefit of being kinetic as well. Obviously, you will not become an expert or perhaps even proficient in any of these endeavors over 30 days, but you will make substantial progress, grow your brain, and hopefully enjoy the hell out of it.

How you go about this is up to you. You can watch videos, take a class, hire an instructor/coach, or even combine a couple modalities.

Master

This challenge is exactly the same as the Apprentice challenge in that you will be learning a new language, musical instrument, or sport – but you will spend at least an hour a day practicing. Yep, that's a huge commitment. That's why it's the Master challenge. If you want to get good at something, do it. Please send me a video of you speaking, playing, or sporting at the end of your month. I want to see you in action. I'm serious!

WORDS OF WISDOM FROM THE BEST...

Nobody has mastered the art of learning like Joshua Waitzkin. In fact, he wrote an incredible book entitled just that: *The Art of Learning*. Joshua was a child prodigy chess champion, and then used his learning chops to become a martial arts champion. For my money he is unrivaled when it comes to the science and art of creating optimal performance. He also happens to be a talented writer.

A few of my favorite Waitzkin gems...

"The fact of the matter is that there will be nothing learned from any challenge in which we don't try our hardest. Growth comes at the point of resistance. We learn by pushing ourselves and finding what really lies at the outer reaches of our abilities".

The real art in learning takes place as we move beyond proficiency, when our work becomes an expression of our essence".

The key to pursuing excellence is to embrace an organic, long-term learning process, and not to live in a shell of static, safe mediocrity. Usually, growth comes at the expense of previous comfort or safety".

RECOMMENDED READING

Newport, Cal. *Deep Work: Rules for Focused Success in a Distracted World*. Grand Central Publishing, 2016.

Gladwell, Malcolm. *Outliers: The Story of Success*. Little, Brown and Company, 2008

Waitzkin, Josh. *The Art of Leaning: An Inner Journey of Optimal Performance.* The Free Press, 2007.

Lewis, Benny. *Fluent in 3 Months: How Anyone at Any Age Can Learn to Speak Any Language from Anywhere in the World.* HarperOne, 2014.

CHALLENGE 7 - REFLECTIONS

Please take a few minutes to think about the past 30 days and answer these questions. Write them down someplace where you can come back and revisit your thoughts.

What were the key takeaways from this month?

What (if anything) do I plan to incorporate into my life moving forward?

What is the next big thing I'm excited to learn?

MONTH 8

CHALLENGE: STILLNESS
SPIRITUAL/SERVICE/CONTRIBUTION

Meditation is the best. Of course, I didn't always feel that way. Nowadays meditation has become part of the mainstream lexicon and is a staple of CEO's and movie-stars alike (along with yoga, $17 juices, and micro-dosing hallucinogens). But back when I was a kid it was some strange and rarely discussed ritual that belonged to monks and shamans. It wasn't until early last decade that I finally decided to really give it a try.

At first, it was scary and uncomfortable. I worried about "getting it right" and quickly became frustrated by my over-active brain. And every time I would try to quiet my mind it would laugh at me and run away. I would try it for a bit, and then lose interest and buzz like a bee to another pretty flower. Until one day I just decided to let go. To give in to the experience and not try so hard. To release the need to be or do anything special. To simply be. Because at its heart that's what meditation is. It is the essence of non-pursuit.

I began to sit quietly every day. Even when I didn't feel like it. *Especially* when I didn't feel like it. I experimented with different techniques and even a couple of phone apps. I used mantras, guided meditations, chanting, and simply silence. But I showed up every day. And slowly my brain began to change in noticeable and wonderful ways. I had more patience. I smiled a lot as it was, but I think I felt my smile deeper (if that makes any sense). And perhaps most notably, I began to experience space between the world and my reaction to it. When a driver cut me off in traffic or a client failed to follow through on a commitment, rather than the normal rush of adrenaline and frustration I felt... peace. I actually felt a tangible space and I could choose how I wanted to respond instead of fall slave to my emotions and patterns. And this is like a key to another world.

This space I speak of eventually happens for all consistent meditators. In my opinion it is the reason to keep coming back. It simply gives you powerful choice in your life. And it's not magic. It is brain wiring. When you sit and concentrate on your breathing, a mantra, or a picture in your mind, it trains your brain to focus on that instead of other things. And when you practice bringing your wandering mind back (because that is what happens) it further trains your brain.

My favorite morning read, *365 Tao* by Deng Ming-Dao, simplifies meditation perfectly:

"The key to any meditation is to concentrate the mind into a single point. There are many methods for doing this, from singing, to listening to holy words, to contemplative procedures. But the end result is the same: To focus our minds sharply.

A mind that is not focused is dispersed over a wide area. Its thoughts are scattered, its energies are in disarray, and it cannot move clearly in any direction. A mind that is clearly focused, however, receives all things and can abide in utter tranquility. It no longer has to chase after all that appears before it".

NOVICE

10 Minutes of box breathing every day. All this requires is your focus. Inhale for a count of 5. Hold the breath for a count of 5. Exhale for a count of 5. Inhale for a count of 5. Repeat. Building a box of breath.

There are many names and origins for this practice, but I first learned it from my dad, uber psychologist Chris Mathe as a simple way to calm yourself and fall asleep. Commander Mark Divine, former Navy seal and founder of SealFit and The Unbeatable Mind Academy also uses and teaches the same technique as a way to stay calm and focused in challenging situations. This rhythm also happens to very closely match the most health promoting pace for inhaling oxygen and exhaling carbon dioxide as outlined in James Nestor's brilliant book *Breath*.

APPRENTICE

21 minutes of meditation every day, broken up into three phases to activate different parts of your brain and body systems (to really get into this I highly recommend *Think Like a Monk* by actual monk Jay Shetty)

Phase 1: 7 minutes of box breathing (see Novice challenge)

Phase 2: 7 minutes of sense visualization
Picture a happy scene from your past or something you'd
like to manifest in the future. In your mind's eye...

See 5 things
Touch 4 things
Hear 3 things
Smell 2 things
Taste 1 thing

For instance, maybe you picture yourself having a picnic
with your spouse. Perhaps you see your spouse's smiling
face, the checkered pattern of the blanket you're sitting on,
the vibrant blue of the sky, the willow wisps hanging over
your heads, and the condensation on the wine bottle. You
touch your spouse's hand, the blades of grass next to you,
the chilled wine glass, the sunshine on your skin. You hear
birds singing to each other, your spouse's laugh, the wind
rustling the leaves. You smell the tang of the gouda and
spring on the air. You taste a strawberry.

This may be challenging at first but have patience with
yourself as your brain learns how to do this. And don't
worry if you don't see clear pictures – some people "see" in
fleeting images and feelings more than 3D pictures. That's
OK.

Phase 3: 7 minutes reciting a mantra or affirmation
Mantra is a Sanskrit word derived from "Man" (mind) and
"Tra (release). It is a syllable, word, or phrase that you
repeat over and over through chanting, singing, speaking, or
even just soundlessly in your head. Focusing on the mantra

frees your mind and allows you to be more receptive and present with the moment.

I like to add a little juice to this exercise by repeating a positive affirmation as the mantra. Something that I would like to affirm about myself or the world. I encourage you to play with this, do some research, and find (or write) your own mantras and affirmations. Maybe you stick with one for a few days. Maybe you cycle through a few. Here are a handful I've used:

So hum (I am)
I am light
I am love
Om
I create for the joy of sharing

You may be wondering – if I am meditating, how do I know 7 minutes has passed and that it's time to move on to the next exercise? Valid point. You can either set an unobtrusive alarm like a bell or chime or use my preferred method which is to just do it by feel. You may be surprised to learn your body is very good at telling time without a clock. It won't be 7 minutes exactly, but that's not important. The point is to spend significant time in each state.

Master
Complete the 21-minute Apprentice challenge PLUS Complete a 30-minute Loving Kindness Meditation every day. I suggest doing one early in the morning and one before bed, but it's up to you where you fit them in. It's probably a good idea to complete them at the same time each day though to deepen the habit groove.

Loving Kindness is an incredible meditation that will generate deep and profound feelings of connection and compassion – both of which are strongly correlated with happiness. Seriously, combining these two meditations for 30 days straight is going to be epic! High level monk brain training in the comfort of your own home. Love it.

Loving Kindness meditations can be found many places, but the following exercise was taken from the organization Greater Good In Action and was created by researcher Emma Seppala, Science Director of Stanford University's Center for Compassion and Altruism Research and Education.

Here is how to practice your Loving Kindness meditation (This is going to span a few pages, but it's actually very simple so try not to get overwhelmed):

Body Position
Close your eyes. Sit comfortably with your feet flat on the floor and your spine straight. Relax your whole body. Keep your eyes closed throughout the whole visualization and bring your awareness inward. Without straining or concentrating, just relax and gently follow the instructions.
Take a deep breath in. And breathe out.

Receiving Loving-Kindness
Keeping your eyes closed, think of a person close to you who loves you very much. It could be someone from the past or the present; someone still in life or who has passed; it could be a spiritual teacher or guide. Imagine that person standing on your right side, sending you their love. That person is sending you wishes for your safety, for your well-being and

happiness. Feel the warm wishes and love coming from that person towards you.

Now bring to mind the same person or another person who cherishes you deeply. Imagine that person standing on your left side, sending you wishes for your wellness, for your health and happiness. Feel the kindness and warmth coming to you from that person.

Now imagine that you are surrounded on all sides by all the people who love you and have loved you. Picture all of your friends and loved ones surrounding you. They are standing sending you wishes for your happiness, well-being, and health. Bask in the warm wishes and love coming from all sides. You are filled and overflowing with warmth and love.

Sending Loving-Kindness to Loved Ones
Now bring your awareness back to the person standing on your right side. Begin to send the love that you feel back to that person. You and this person are similar. Just like you, this person wishes to be happy. Send all your love and warm wishes to that person.

Repeat the following phrases, silently:
May you live with ease, may you be happy, may you be free from pain.
May you live with ease, may you be happy, may you be free from pain.
May you live with ease, may you be happy, may you be free from pain.

Now focus your awareness on the person standing on your left side. Begin to direct the love within you to that person.

Send all your love and warmth to that person. That person and you are alike. Just like you, that person wishes to have a good life.

Repeat the following phrases, silently:
Just as I wish to, may you be safe, may you be healthy, may you live with ease and happiness.
Just as I wish to, may you be safe, may you be healthy, may you live with ease and happiness.
Just as I wish to, may you be safe, may you be healthy, may you live with ease and happiness.

Now picture another person that you love, perhaps a relative or a friend. This person, like you, wishes to have a happy life. Send warm wishes to that person.

Repeat the following phrases, silently:
May your life be filled with happiness, health, and well-being.
May your life be filled with happiness, health, and well-being.
May your life be filled with happiness, health, and well-being.

Sending Loving-Kindness to Neutral People

Now think of an acquaintance, someone you don't know very well and toward whom you do not have any particular feeling. You and this person are alike in your wish to have a good life.
Send all your wishes for well-being to that person, repeating the following phrases, silently:

Just as I wish to, may you also live with ease and happiness.

Just as I wish to, may you also live with ease and happiness.
Just as I wish to, may you also live with ease and happiness.

Now bring to mind another acquaintance toward whom you feel neutral. It could be a neighbor, or a colleague, or someone else that you see around but do not know very well. Like you, this person wishes to experience joy and well-being in his or her life.

Send all your good wishes to that person, repeating the following phrases, silently:
May you be happy, may you be healthy, may you be free from all pain.
May you be happy, may you be healthy, may you be free from all pain.
May you be happy, may you be healthy, may you be free from all pain.

Sending Loving-Kindness to All Living Beings
Now expand your awareness and picture the whole globe in front of you as a little ball.
Send warm wishes to all living beings on the globe, who, like you, want to be happy:
Just as I wish to, may you live with ease, happiness, and good health.
Just as I wish to, may you live with ease, happiness, and good health.
Just as I wish to, may you live with ease, happiness, and good health.

Take a deep breath in. And breathe out. And another deep breath in and let it go. Notice the state of your mind and how you feel after this meditation.

When you're ready, you may open your eyes.

That's it. Simple, but outright rocket-fuel for your brain and spirit.

Words of wisdom from the best...
Andy Puddicombe is the co-founder of the revolutionary meditation app Headspace. He is a former Buddhist monk who is passionate about meditation and bringing it to as many people as possible. I find his wisdom simple, refreshing, and humble. Some of Andy's thoughts about meditation:

"Best advice ever received was from one of my meditation teachers at the monastery: 'Be present, be patient, be gentle, be kind...everything else will take care of itself'".

"Meditation and life are not separate. Meditation simply helps us to see and understand life more clearly".

"In letting go, we cease trying to make something happen, and then the mind naturally opens. It is like watching a flower grow — free from effort, its petals naturally unfold to reveal its beauty".

Recommended reading
Shetty, Jay. *Think Like a Monk: Train Your Mind for Peace and Purpose Everyday*. Simon & Schuster, 2020.

Dispenza, Joe. *Becoming Supernatural: How Common People are Doing the Uncommon*. Hay House Inc, 2017.

Divine, Mark. *Unbeatable Mind: Forging Resiliency and*

Mental Toughness to Succeed at an Elite Level. Mark Divine, 3rd Edition, 2015.

Nestor, James. *Breath: The New Science of a Lost Art*. Riverhead Books, 2020.

Deng, Ming-Dao. *365 Tao: Daily Meditations*. HarperOne, 1991.

CHALLENGE 8 - REFLECTIONS

Please take a few minutes to think about the past 30 days and answer these questions. Write them down someplace where you can come back and revisit your thoughts.

What were the key takeaways from this month?

What (if anything) do I plan to incorporate into my life moving forward?

Can I sense the space between what happens and my reaction to it?

CHALLENGE: QUALITY TIME
FAMILY/FRIENDS/RELATIONSHIPS

Have you ever spent time with someone who knows they are living the last days of their life? This is obviously a difficult time for all involved, but they also often contain exquisite moments of clarity. Never, like EVER, do these folks express regret about not making more money, having more things, or starting more companies. Instead, they talk about friendships, children, spouses, and...love. The times they most cherish (and regret if they came to this realization late in life) almost always center around connection. That shared oneness and special bond that happens when I see you and you see me.

Actively choosing to live life as if you know you're dying (because, well, you are) is what my dad likes to call being "coffin ready". That may sound morbid but it's also freeing. If you have said all that needs to be said to those that need to hear it, loved hard and deeply, and thrown yourself into the arena over and over again even when you are terrified – everything else is gravy. Whether you move on to the next great adventure tomorrow or in 300 years (I suffer from major immortality fantasies. What? It could happen), at least you know you are ready. Mountains climbed, houses flipped, hands won, and first-class flights can all be fun stops along the way, but completely superfluous for happiness and foundational contentment.

You know the phrase "show me your calendar and I'll show you what's important to you"? Perhaps a bit trite, but bluntly accurate. Yes, I know your sister knows you love her and your best friend knows how much she means to you. But when was the last time you said these things out loud? Or better yet, took time out of your busy life to SHOW them how special they are? It is the people that you love and that love you, that mean everything. Everything. This month you are going to show them that, every day.

Novice

Have an IN PERSON meal and/or conversation with someone you care about three times a week, for a total of 12 times over these 30 days. No phones, TV, or distractions. Pay attention with an open heart, mind, and ears. Try not to partially listen while planning your response. Make eye contact. Not required but highly recommended is to purposely choose topics of discussion that contain depth (it can be tough to build connection if you are dishing about what a Kardashian said on Instagram).

Apprentice

Complete the Novice challenge AND include 2 adventures this month with people that you care about. I will let you interpret what "adventure" means to you in this context, but let fun be your guide. When we take the time and space to spend time with others while engaging in sensory experiences it is like drinking connection through a firehose. Go wine tasting, tandem kayak to an island, hike to a hilltop with paints and easels, or tour your city's underground tunnels. Your imagination is the limit. Although you can steal other people's ideas too. Do an internet search for interesting things to do in your area. Or not your area. I have a friend that flew his wife to Chicago for lunch.

MASTER
Complete both the Novice and Apprentice challenges PLUS include an overnight trip with someone you care about sometime over the next 30 days. This overnight trip is in addition to the 2 adventures you're having with special people, and it must include at least one evening away from home. Like engaging in sensory activities, simply being away from home and in a new environment lights up your spirit in a way that facilitates connection. This can be as simple as a camping excursion or as fancy as a whirlwind trip to sample the fondue in Switzerland. But don't get so distracted by the trappings that you lose the forest for the trees. The point is simple, real time with someone you care about. You can do that with Michelin star dinners if you want to, but you can achieve the same thing with a box of Mac & Cheese.

WORDS OF WISDOM FROM THE BEST...
In Viktor Frankl's haunting classic *Man's Search for Meaning* (about his time spent in a Nazi concentration camp. I recommended this book during Challenge 5) he explores why we are here, what is fundamentally important, and how to truly live.

"For the first time in my life I saw the truth as it is set into song by so many poets, proclaimed as the final wisdom by so many thinkers. The truth - that Love is the ultimate and highest goal to which man can aspire. Then I grasped the meaning of the greatest secret that human poetry and human thought and belief have to impart: The salvation of man is through love and in love".

Recommended Reading

Albom, Mitch. *Tuesdays with Morrie: An Old Man, a Young Man, and Life's Greatest Lesson*. Crown, 20th Anniversary Reprint, 2007.

Muller, Wayne. *How Then Shall We Live? Four Simple Questions that Reveal the Beauty and Meaning of our Lives*. Bantam, 1996.

Gawande, Atul. *Being Mortal: Medicine and What Matters in the End*. Metropolitan Books, 2014.

CHALLENGE 9 - REFLECTIONS

Please take a few minutes to think about the past 30 days and answer these questions. Write them down someplace where you can come back and revisit your thoughts.

What were the key takeaways from this month?

What (if anything) do I plan to incorporate into my life moving forward?

What is my life about and why am I here? What makes my soul sing?

MONTH 10

CHALLENGE: TAME THE MONSTER
PHYSICAL/NUTRITION/HEALTH

Fasting has become all the rage over the last few years, and for good reason. It looks to be extremely good for health, longevity, and weight loss. This cascade of benefits occurs by flipping on your body's stem cells, which can regenerate organs and systems thereby reducing or even reversing disease. From a hormonal perspective, fasting is the switch flipper. (For data driven folks, the books at the end of the chapter are great resources)

There are a plethora of ways to fast, but for this challenge we are going to focus on my favorite – both in terms of expected results and easy application. And if the idea of going multiple hours without feeding your stomach monster scares you, the good news is that you are already a fasting expert (you do it nightly while sleeping. That's where the word break-fast comes from). We are just going to push back that window a little.

This challenge will be awesome no matter who you are or where you are with your health. If you have weight to lose, you will - but even more than that will be the health, longevity, and discipline benefits. Another opportunity to consciously claim your food decisions.

NOVICE

Complete a daily 12 hour fast. That means after dinner you don't eat again until the following day 12 hours later. If you have dinner at 7 PM, you don't eat again until breakfast the next day at 7 AM. This is actually very do-able and many people regularly accomplish it accidentally. The difference is that you are going to do it mindfully, EVERY-DAY. It also means no late-night snacking which is huge for many people. When I first started doing this I quickly had to accept the fact that not ingesting calories after dinner meant no beer or snacking while watching baseball, accounting for a solid 500-800 calories a day!

APPRENTICE

Complete a daily 14 hour fast. That means after dinner you don't eat again until the following day 14 hours later. If you have dinner at 7 PM, you don't eat again until the following day at 9 AM. This will be a little harder than the 12-hour fast but my experience is that it quickly becomes easy. Your body gets accustomed to the longer window and you probably won't even experience much hunger or discomfort.

Part 2 of this challenge is to start the day with cup of coffee and a brisk 30-45 minute walk (you can even combine these as I do. Also, the caffeine in coffee gives a little metabolic boost, but no worries if you don't drink coffee. You can choose tea, or nothing at all) I would not be surprised if this becomes the favorite part of your day. It is extremely centering to immerse yourself in the mundane beauty of this routine. After a time you will also notice that you become more aware of the seasons and world around you. You will be there when that first winter breeze arrives, when the leaves begin to fall, and when the spring buds cautiously start to emerge. It's fantastic. Oh, and you may just become a lean, mean, 6-packed machine.

Master
Complete a daily 16 hour fast (which looks to be ideal for the hormonal benefits we are trying to trigger). That means after dinner you don't eat again until the following day 16 hours later, generally about lunchtime. If you have dinner at 7 PM, you don't eat again until the following day at 11 AM.   This tends to be a bit harder for people, especially those who are accustomed to eating every few hours. But, like all things your body adapts and becomes more efficient at using the energy it has already stored – which will eventually minimize hunger and maximize leanness.

Part 2 of this challenge is to start the day with a cup of coffee and a brisk 30-45 minute like Apprentice challenge PLUS move every hour of the day.

Most of us sit for extended periods of time each day, even those of us who consider ourselves athletes. That has some major and well documented deleterious health effects - most notably premature death! Counteract that by setting an alarm to go off every hour between 8-5 and then doing some form of movement/exercise when you hear it. No matter what. 20 squats, 15 pushups, 5 pull-ups, 30 crunches, 20 lunges, 10 jump squats, 10 burpees, etc. Heck go for a 15 minute walk if you're feeling inspired. The key is to complete this regardless of whatever else you're doing. If you're on a conference call, do some squats while you listen. If you're driving, pull over and bang out some jumping jacks. It actually becomes a game. If people look at you funny when you start doing lunges on a Zoom chat just remind yourself that they are jealous of your discipline and awesomeness!

Part 3 of this challenge is to complete a full 24 hour fast once a week. Plan ahead and do these a full 7 days apart from each other. Also, look at your schedule for the month (as best you can) and decide where these should go. Week-ends are often best because it makes sense to do this over a day when you won't be required to engage in anything physically or mentally demanding.   During this time, you can drink as much water as you want (and other non-caloric beverages like tea). You can also have some bone or vegetable broth if you're feeling a little peckish. This isn't easy, but the science is emerging and the health benefits, weight loss benefits, and mental benefits look to be prodi-gious. Just proving to yourself you can do this is extremely empowering in its own right.

WORDS OF WISDOM FROM THE BEST...
Valter Longo is a biogerontologist and cell biologist who serves as the director for the USC Longevity Institute. Dr. Longo has quite literally spent his entire adult life studying how and why humans age and is arguably the world's leading longevity expert. For anyone interested in living a long, healthy, active life – this is the man to pay attention to.

"[Fasting] I have discovered can protect, regenerate, and rejuvenate the body to keep us young and healthy longer.

[Fasting] is also clinically proven to stimulate the loss of abdominal fat while conserving muscle and bone mass".

Dr. Longo also makes a crucial point regarding longevity: "It's not just the idea of living longer that has driven me; it's living healthy longer".

I could not agree more. Whenever I talk to people about my dreams of living hundreds of years their eyes get wide and they back away from me in terror. I never understood this reaction until I realized they were imagining nursing homes, walkers, cannulas, pain, and suffering. I don't want this either! What I want for you, and me, and humanity is exactly what Dr. Longo is describing. A long, healthy, strong, vibrant life; where you pass away during a nap after an awesome brunch and a surfing lesson.

RECOMMENDED READING

Longo, Valter. *The Longevity Diet: Discover the New Science Behind Stem Cell Activation and Regeneration to Slow Aging, Fight Disease, and Optimize Weight*. Avery, 2018.

Greenfield, Ben. *Boundless: Upgrade Your Brain, Optimize Your Body & Defy Aging*. Victory Belt Publishing, 2020.

Walford, Roy M.D. *Beyond the 120 Year Diet: How to Double Your Vital Years*. Thunder's Mouth Press, 2000.

CHALLENGE 10 - REFLECTIONS

Please take a few minutes to think about the past 30 days and answer these questions. Write them down someplace where you can come back and revisit your thoughts.

What were the key takeaways from this month?

What (if anything) do I plan to incorporate into my life moving forward?

What did I learn about my body and hunger during this challenge?

MONTH 11

CHALLENGE: ADD AN ARROW
TO YOUR QUIVER
CAREER/BUSINESS/FINANCIAL

Are you exactly where you want to be in your career? Probably not, as most people (especially Americans) resoundingly answer this question negatively. If you happen to love your career and your place in it, good for you! Either way, there are always new skills to be learned that can make you better at your current job, or more equipped for a job you actually want. And no free passes if you're retired! One of the things I absolutely love about where we are at this point in history is that older folks are living with the same passion and purpose as young hustlers trying to make their mark. It may look different, but we don't just stop caring because our primary career has finished. In fact, older people generally have a more robust perspective on happiness and a much deeper (and often more honest) relationship with themselves. If this describes you, you get to have some extra fun with this challenge.

For all of us, it can be challenging to take the time, energy, and bandwidth to focus on yourself while you are busy just trying to accomplish the tasks of your life. We get so lost working IN the business of our jobs and lives that we fail to give time and space to the actual essence OF our jobs and lives; we become human DOINGS rather than human BEINGS. And this cycle will continue unabated unless you actively and unapologetically claim time and energy for sharpening your saw.

Novice

Identify and practice a critical skill that would make you better/more efficient/more marketable at your current job OR a career you would like to transition to. Spend 15 minutes each day making yourself even more exceptional. (Clarification point: I am specifically challenging you to improve a skill – not take on a new degree or certification. You can do that if it makes sense in your life plan, but it doesn't satisfy the challenge requirements)

What are your opportunity areas in this regard? Public speaking? Writing? Time management? Computer programming? Once you have identified and selected your target for the month, decide how you are going to practice and improve. If you'd like to become a better speaker, perhaps you sign up for toastmasters or videotape yourself giving speeches and then send them to a trusted friend or an expert for constructive feedback. If you'd like to improve your writing, you can start by simply committing to writing something every day. Time management practice might look like taking time each day to critically evaluate your commitments and goals and time block your calendar.

Whatever you choose and however you choose to do it, your challenge is to spend 15 minutes each day doing something to enhance your chosen skill. Something else I should mention because it is surprisingly important - choose an area of opportunity that excites you. Life is too short to spend large amounts of time doing things that suck. Make this pleasurable and gratifying. If you can't find the fun, perhaps it's time explore other careers.

APPRENTICE

Like the Novice challenge, you are going to identify and practice a critical skill that would make you better/more efficient/more marketable at your current job OR a career you would like to transition to – but you will spend 30 *minutes each day* making yourself even more exceptional.

Also, let's make the education a bit more structured by actually signing up for a class or some kind of formal training. If the Novice commits to writing 15 minutes a day, you are going to commit to taking a writing class as well as writing every day. Spend at least 30 minutes daily improving your skill.

MASTER

Same basic starting point: Identify and practice a critical skill that would make you better/more efficient/more marketable at your current job OR a career you would like to transition to – but you will spend *at least an hour each day* making yourself even more exceptional.

Also, as a master you will find a mentor or hire a coach and work with them on improving the specific skill you have identified. You may already have someone in your life that can serve as a mentor in a particular area, but often finding someone like this takes some doing. Think about your network. Is there someone you respect that you would like to learn from? Reach out, tell them exactly what you are doing and why, and ask them if they'd be willing to help you. Almost always, people at the top of their professions are more than happy to give back and share their accumulated wisdom. The reason for this is often threefold: it feels good to be acknowledged; they are aware of and grateful for the help they received in their own journeys; successful people worthy of your respect generally have a giving spirit.

If there isn't anyone in your network that feels like mentor material, cast a wider net. There are so many experts that we have almost instant access to now. If you want to improve time management, how about emailing the author of a best-selling time management book and asking her to help you? This may sound crazy, but people love to help! And remember – they are just people. After I released my first book, I emailed a few well-known people to see if I could send them copies. The loose agenda was to get endorsements, but mostly I was just excited about my book and wanted to share it. As uncomfortable as that was, almost all of them responded positively and the most famous of them all was incredibly gracious and has become a friend. People are just people.

Of course, you can also hire an actual coach whose job it is to help people just like you. I am a huge fan of working with a coach to improve any number of things in your life. Plus, we are firmly entrenched in the golden age of coaching. With a few keystrokes and clicks you can find a host of coaches that will be happy to teach you, quite literally, anything. Don't just hire anyone though. Do your homework. What relevant education and experience do they have? Will they provide references? Do they have a coaching philosophy that they can coherently articulate? Interview them and make sure you vibe. Also, expect to pay for what you get. A good coach isn't cheap. If they are willing to coach you for way under market value, that should be a flashing neon red flag.

Once you have added a mentor or coach to your team, create guidelines and ground rules for your relationship. How are they going to help you and hold you accountable? Will you be required to provide deliverables? How will your learning and growth be measured? What does success look like? What exactly are the expectations on both sides?

Spend at least an hour a day mastering your chosen skill.

* A note for retirees: If you are retired, use these challenges to become more proficient at a skill that will benefit a primary passion area for you, or an area you'd like to bring into your life. Do you volunteer at an animal shelter? Perhaps they could really use someone with spreadsheet mastery. Have you always wanted to paint? Maybe now is the time to start honing your craft. You are in a wonderful position of increased bandwidth so you can really dive in to endeavors like this!

WORDS OF WISDOM FROM THE BEST...
Cal Newport is a computer science professor at Georgetown University, and the New York Times bestselling author of seven books including one of my favorites, *Deep Work*. He is one of those people that sees the world differently and stretches your paradigm in a deliciously uncomfortable way.

"Passion comes after you put in the hard work to become excellent at something valuable, not before. In other words, what you do for a living is much less important than how you do it." But then later, "If you want to love what you do, abandon the passion mindset ("what can the world offer me?") and instead adopt the craftsman mindset ("what can I offer the world?")." This may seem contradictory, but I think he's saying go ahead and be passionate but don't make your work about you. Make it about service.

RECOMMENDED READING
Leonard, George. *Mastery: The Keys to Success and Long-Term Fulfillment*. Plume, 1992.

Ferriss, Tim. *Tools of Titans: The Tactics, Routines, and Habits of Billionaires, Icons, and World-Class Performers*. Mariner Books, 2016.

Ferriss, Tim. *Tribe of Mentors: Short Life Advice from the Best in the World*. Mariner Books, 2017.

A book about the specific skill you are trying to improve?

CHALLENGE 11 - REFLECTIONS

Please take a few minutes to think about the past 30 days and answer these questions. Write them down someplace where you can come back and revisit your thoughts.

What were the key takeaways from this month?

What (if anything) do I plan to incorporate into my life moving forward?

Does being engaged in the learning process contribute to feelings of happiness and/or purpose for me?

MONTH 12

CHALLENGE: BIG ROCK
ADVENTURE/LIFESTYLE

There is incredible power in going after something that scares us. The whole arc of that decision has been fundamental to the human experience since the beginning of time. You get the twinkling of an idea that a mammoth might provide food for the entire clan through the winter. Then, the period of incredulity while you kick the idea around in your brain. The cautious optimism you bring to telling others about it. The building burn of excitement as you realize it could actually happen. The quiet determination as you plan and prepare. The despair when it seems as if it will be impossible. Finally, the surge of adrenaline and triumph as the mammoth falls to the ground. We achievers (I know you're an achiever because you're reading this book) are very familiar with this process. It may even be one of the defining cycles of our lives. However, since humans are so wonderfully paradoxical, we also tend to stick to our comfort zones.

This challenge is about finding new and different things to go after. Not because you aren't OK without achievement or to fill some indefinable hole inside you, but because you can, because it will be a blast, and it will help you learn more about yourself and life.

The challenge for this month is to go after a Big Rock. What do I mean by that? Well, it could be a literal Big. Rock. Like El Capitan or Mt. Everest, but it is meant as a metaphor for something enormous and seemingly unattainable. Something that scares you and excites you (have you noticed this is a theme?). Something that you almost don't want to put down on paper or tell anyone about because it seems so ridiculous. In fact, I want that to be your guiding principle. Start with ridiculous and go from there. This month we are going to internalize the simple truth that we all are capable of so much more than we think we are.

Big Rocks will be different for all of us of course. Singing on stage in front of thousands of people would be a HUGE rock for me. I can barely even imagine it. But Paul McCartney would do this before lunch without raising his heart rate. So, what's a Big Rock for you?

Novice
Pick a Big Rock that is out of your comfort zone. Train for 30 minutes a day to achieve it. Pick something that can be completed by the end of the month. What do I mean by "train"? Practice, specific to your goal. Training can be physical, mental, emotional, or spiritual. In fact, it should probably be a combination of all of them. When I decided to run the John Muir Trail my training included trail running, but also visualization, gratitude, meditation, and a lot of study and planning.

APPRENTICE

Pick a Big Rock that is out of your comfort zone. Train for 45 minutes a day to achieve it. If the actual attainment/completion of your Big Rock falls in this month, great – but it doesn't have to. I realize that if you are training to swim the English channel (one of my Big Rocks. I talked to a coach that says I'm simply not a fast enough swimmer but I haven't fully accepted that yet) it will not fall in the next 30 days unless you've already been preparing. That's OK. Choose your Big Rock and begin training for it this month. Continue until your Big Rock has been achieved!

MASTER

Pick a GIGANTIC ROCK that makes you want to pee your pants and thrills you all at the same time. Train for at least an hour a day to achieve it. If you are going for Master here you better be ready to party. This isn't just about training more, but about shooting higher. At this level you've probably already done some things other people would consider crazy. Good. Go bigger. I'm not advocating life threatening, just way out of your comfort zone or normal world. This could be a monumental physical challenge like a 100-mile running race. It could take the form of a spiritual reckoning like a multi-week silent retreat (fun to think about what your training would be for this). It can really be anything as long as it speaks to your soul. Be creative. Be bold. Be the most YOU you can be. And like Apprentice, this Big Rock doesn't have to fall during the challenge month. Just keep training.

*For Apprentice and Master – if your Big Rock doesn't fall in the month of the challenge make sure to give yourself a test/celebration at the 30-day mark.

Words of wisdom from the best...

David Goggins is an incredible human being. After an extremely difficult childhood and obese beginnings, he became a Navy Seal - completing BUDS (Basic Underwater Demolition/SEAL training, widely considered to be the most difficult military training on the planet) with broken legs. He then became a top endurance runner, racing hundreds of miles at one time. Now a retired SEAL, he spends his time writing best-selling books and fighting wildfires for fun. I often ask myself WWDD (What Would David Do) when working with a coaching client or trying to push myself up a hill. He has trained his mind and body to a point few humans have ever been, and most wouldn't even consider possible. A living embodiment of the essence of this challenge, David is always exploring the boundaries of reality and comfort.

Here is a sampling of some unadulterated Goggins.

"You are in danger of living a life so comfortable and soft, that you will die without ever realizing your true potential".

"We're either getting better or we're getting worse".

"Don't focus on what you think you deserve. Take aim at what you are willing to earn".

"I don't stop when I'm tired, I stop when I'm done".

"From the time you take your first breath, you become eligible to die. You also become eligible to find your greatness".

Love me some Goggins.

RECOMMENDED READING
Goggins, David. *Can't Hurt Me: Master Your Mind and Defy the Odds*. Lioncrest Publishing, 2018.

Itzler, Jesse. *Living with a SEAL: 31 Days Training with the Toughest Man on the Planet*. Center Street, 2015.
(This is a fun book about a guy who hired David Goggins to live with him for a month)

Lansing, Albert. *Endurance: Shackleton's Incredible Voyage*. Basic Books, Anniversary Edition, 2014.

Hoad, Richard, et al. *The World's Toughest Endurance Challenges*. Velo Press, 2012.

Caldwell, Tommy. *The Push: A Climber's Search for the Path*. Penguin Books, 2017.

Mathe, Josh. *I, Athlete: How to unleash your inner athlete and supercharge your life!* Mountain Ninja Publishing, 2017.

You may have guessed that I love this challenge! If you would indulge me, please email me letting me know what your Big Rocks are and when you've completed them!

CHALLENGE 12 - REFLECTIONS

Please take a few minutes to think about the past 30 days and answer these questions. Write them down someplace where you can come back and revisit your thoughts.

What were the key takeaways from this month?

What (if anything) do I plan to incorporate into my life moving forward?

If I set aside fear, judgement, expectations, time, and money - what is the BIGGEST ROCK I can dream up?

CONCLUSION

"BONG: Thanks again for flying Discipline Airlines. You are now free to move about the cabin to find your greatness..."

Well, we've made it to the end my friends! I have split this chapter into two parts based on how you decided to move through the book. As I said in the introduction, I wanted this to be a "Choose Your Own Adventure" experience. With that said...

1. If you just finished this book and have yet to go back and start the challenges, continue reading below.

2. If you have already completed the challenges, skip ahead to the next section.

1. I just finished the book and now I'm ready to start Challenge 1!

Boy are you in for a rousing year! I put the Big Rock challenge last and left you with David Goggins on purpose. Are you walking the balance beam between panic and excitement? Is your mind reeling and your face smiling? Perfect.

Comfortable is so boring. The masses seek comfort. They go to the same restaurants, spend time with the same people, and go to the same jobs. Day after day, year after year. They shy away from hard things, flip on their televisions, and tell themselves they will do something interesting tomorrow. But that is not you.

You are a warrior poet born in the wrong century, yearning to make your mark on your life. It's not about achievement, or trophies, or what anyone else thinks. It is about the unyielding voice of your spirit urging you forward. Your best life is waiting just down the path in front of you. All you need to do is step forward.

I know there is a park bench off the path that looks inviting. Walk past it. I know there are people behind you complaining about your pace and asking you to slow down. Ignore them. I know the sun on the horizon is so bright that it scares you. That's OK. Just keep walking.

All of the lessons in this book are exponentially positive, fitting together and expanding like Legos of life. Place one Lego at a time, building your house of discipline - and when you open the door and walk inside you will find more badassery and happiness than you ever thought possible.

Sure, it will be hard. It will absolutely make you grow. And it will be one heck of a ride. Enjoy!

2. I just finished the book and have completed all the challenges!

Whew, what a year! We have spent the last 12 months together and you have accomplished some incredible things! Big time virtual fist bump from me to you.

This year you...

1. Read your tuchus off
2. Got your grateful on
3. Channeled Indiana Jones
4. Showed sugar who is boss
5. Deeply connected with people you love
6. Took financial leaps forward
7. Learned A LOT
8. Became Buddhaesque
9. Did some awesome things with awesome people
10. Tamed your hunger
11. Mastered a new skill
12. Scaled a Big Rock

My hope is from now on when you see the word "discipline" you no longer think of a drill sergeant and starched trousers, but rather smile and shake your head because you know the truth. That discipline is simply your secret weapon to living life exactly the way you want to. And that it can actually be fun!

Take out your Reflections journal and look back on how far you have come and what you learned during each of these challenges. How are you different in this moment than you were when you started reading this book? How has your personal definition of "discipline" evolved? If you are feeling frisky jot down your final thoughts in your journal. Remember, you can always come back to this bible of wisdom you have created.

I would also like to invite you to use this book till it's worn and tattered rather than throwing it on a shelf and forgetting about it. In the introduction I mentioned that you could theoretically complete the challenges in this book three times over three years, and I meant it. Go back and repeat challenges at increased levels of skill and commitment. Growth isn't about starting or finishing - it's about the space in between. So keep exploring that space as long as it feels like a value add!

Lastly, don't be an island. Find accountability partners. Share your successes and struggles with friends and family. Reach out to coaches and mentors. Email me with questions and pictures of you standing on mountain tops. Change is easier, stickier, and more fun when you engage others in the process.

Thank you for joining me on this grand adventure!

The End. And the beginning...

AUTHOR'S NOTES

As with most writers, it is so hard for me to choose a topic to dive into with enough focus and discipline (I am aware of the irony) to actually produce a book. I will get excited by an idea, jot down a few pages of notes, and then move on to the next fun idea. Ideas provide a wonderful dopamine splash that feel good and don't require any effort. Producing a complete book though? That's no joke.

So why this topic rather than the 247 others on my list? Because it is the most actionable. I hope. I truly meant what I said in the introduction. My goal with this book was to give you just enough to wet your appetite and help inspire you to generate movement in your life.

I love change and being along for that ride in people's lives. I imagine that we are bouncing on a raft together while the whitewater crashes against our boat, or that we are slowly climbing craggy stone steps in search of a forgotten Himalayan temple. Change is so difficult but so awesome - this is the fuel that keeps my fire burning.

What's next? A real estate book (one of my many hats), perhaps a deep dive into a couple of the most storied ultra-marathons in the world, maybe even a second version of this book with more challenges! I will let the river take me where it will, but one thing is for certain. I will keep trying to help people tap into the strongest, truest versions of who they are.

Thanks again for joining me and for caring what I have to say. There is always a little fear that nobody will listen, and that is part of the journey too. As I've said many times in this book, please reach out if you have any questions, ideas for cool adventures, or simply to share your successes.

Till next time!

Josh Mathe

ACKNOWLEDGMENTS

The creative process is so interesting in that it can sometimes feel lonely but is truly a community effort. Even the idea for this book came from a conversation I had with my accountability partners.

Thank you Michael Nelson and Lance Loveday for that conversation and for encouraging me to keep plucking away at the keyboard.

Also, a huge thank you to Michael and my mom for helping me work through the book edits. That is never my favorite part of creating a book and you helped immensely.

To my Advanced Reader Team, you are the best! I so much appreciate you being patient with me and cheering me along the way. You have no idea how much a kind word (or simply knowing you were out there waiting for the book) helped me stay engaged and motivated!

Lastly, to my amazing wife. Thank you for giving me the space and support to do this - and all the other things that make my life interesting to me. I couldn't do any of it without the foundation you provide.

SPECIAL INVITATION
YES, AGAIN

To my amazing readers:

Thank you once again for picking up this book and making it to the end! If you haven't already done so I'd like to invite you to grab a free copy of my first book, *In the Footsteps of Greatness*. It is an award winning memoir about running the John Muir Trail in the Sierra Nevada wilderness of California (and who I had to become to get there). Your free copy is waiting below!

https://bit.ly/ITFOGFreeBook

Also, a reminder that inspirational adventures are what I typically write about. If this is your bag please subscribe to my list below. No spam - just special content, fun stuff, random thoughts, and recommendations for other reads you might enjoy.

To your health and happiness!

www.joshmathe.com/mailing-list

PLEASE LEAVE A REVIEW!

Book reviews are one of the best ways to get Amazon algorithms working for a book/author rather than said book vaporizing into the ether. If you enjoyed this book and are willing to take 5 minutes to leave an honest Amazon review I would be much obliged.

Help me avoid vaporization Obi-Wan. You're my only hope!

ABOUT THE AUTHOR

Josh Mathe is passionate about squeezing every last drop from life, and helping others do the same. He is the award-winning author of *In the Footsteps of Greatness* and *I, Athlete*, as well as a speaker, fitness expert, nutritionist, ultra-endurance athlete, and life adventurer. A serial entreprenuer, Josh is the co-owner of One10 Performance and Backyard Real Estate. When not working with individual clients he spends his days running through the wilderness or lifting heavy things. Josh holds a Master's of Science in Human Nutrition, and is a certified sports nutritionist (CISSN), Performance Enhancement Specialist (PES), and endurance coach. He lives in Sacramento, CA with his wife and two crazy dogs.

For more information or to contact Josh directly, please visit www.joshmathe.com

Made in the USA
Monee, IL
30 November 2021